MW01259277

GOD WITH US

A JOURNEY HOME

by Jeremy Pierre

Illustrations by Cassandra Clark

Text © 2020 Jeremy Pierre
Art © 2020 Cassandra Clark
ISBN
Paper: 978-1-633421790
epub: 978-1-633421806
Kindle: 978-1-633421813

Shepherd Press
P.O. Box 24
Wapwallopen, PA 18660
www.shepherdpress.com

Scripture quotations are from the ESV® Bible
(The Holy Bible, English Standard Version®),
copyright © 2001 by Crossway,
a publishing ministry of Good News Publishers.
Used by permission. All rights reserved.

All rights reserved.
No part of this publication may be reproduced,
or stored in a retrieval system,
or transmitted, in any form or by any means,
mechanical, electronic, photocopying, recording or otherwise,
without the prior permission of Shepherd Press.

Printed in India

DEDICATION

To Allie, pardon if I love you more each day.
To Ronnie, rest awaits you on the far side of war.
To Marlie, may your hope shame this gloomy earth.
To Frankie, your eyes were made to see hidden glory.
To Betsie, may you always shine like winter sun.

As delightful as our home is,
may each of you find your home in God.

APPRECIATIONS

"*God with Us: A Journey Home* is a marvelous story Bible for children. It teases out one of the often-undeveloped themes of the Bible—the presence of God. This extraordinary book develops the unfolding drama of God's purpose to bring his children home, home to him. Jeremy Pierre describes the peril of mankind, estranged from God, and the dangers of the journey home. The artistry of Pierre's writing is elegant in its simplicity while being profound in content. Each chapter leaves the reader wishing for more. The evocative word pictures of this book are vividly illustrated by engaging artwork. *God with Us* will be a favorite for parents to read to their children. Each chapter will leave them wanting more."

Tedd Tripp
Author of *Shepherding a Child's Heart*

"The theme of God's presence is the culmination of all of biblical revelation. Our hope is to see God's face and to see him just as he is. This beautifully written book, which is both creative and faithful, takes us on a journey and follows the biblical storyline in doing so. A wonderful book for children and for those of any age. The dazzling illustrations are simply stunning in their beauty. The glory of God's presence is displayed in both the writing and the illustrations found in this work. A book to be read and reread again and again."

Thomas R. Schreiner, Ph.D.
Professor of New Testament Interpretation, The Southern Baptist Theological Seminary

"To take such a big and complex biblical theme like the presence of God and bring it to life is a difficult task. And yet this book not only tells that story well, but it does also so with beauty and clarity. *God with Us*, then, is not just another book to read; it is an invitation into the promise of God's presence that defines and shapes all of the Christian life. Jeremy Pierre has done a masterful job offering all of us—parents and kids alike—not just another story, but a lifestyle for today and for all eternity. That is because there is no greater promise than God with us—and that is why we need this book on our shelves and its truths in our hearts."

Ryan Lister
Professor of Theology, Western Seminary

"This is a beautiful retelling of the most beautiful story ever told. Readers of all ages will fall in love with the words and images on these pages which point to the eternal Word, to the one in whose image we are made."

Karen Swallow Prior

Research Professor of English and Christianity & Culture, Southeastern Baptist Theological Seminary and author of *On Reading Well: Finding the Good Life through Great Books*

"*God with Us* delivers truth with imagination, creativity, and beautiful illustrations. Pierre weaves gospel hope through the Old Testament stories and points the reader forward to the Lamb of God in the stories of the New Testament. The gospel message becomes clearer with every turn of the page. Like a symphony of truth that crescendos to the final fanfare, *God with Us* ends with a finale that connects the gospel dots and offers an invitation to believe. Bravo and well done!"

Marty Machowski

Pastor and author of *The Ology, Wonderful, Long Story Short,* and other Gospel-centered resources for church and home

"The one and only thing I dislike about *God with Us* is that it was published too late for me to read it to my children. But I am carefully setting aside my copy and am already looking forward to someday reading it to my grandchildren. I have every confidence they will enjoy it and benefit from it."

Tim Challies

Writer, Reviewer, and Blogger at challies.com

CONTENTS

ACKNOWLEDGEMENTS

This book was a lot more labor than anyone expected, as most things worth doing are. Here at the end of all things, we would like to acknowledge the people who labored alongside us all the way.

We want to thank Shepherd Press for taking on this rather ambitious project. Specifically, we are grateful for the patient leadership of Aaron Tripp, Rick Irvin, and Jim Holmes. Layout is that final step that makes words and images shine, and Chase Jacobs brought his own creative light to this book. We also want to thank the Pierre Family Foundation for its support of this resource, and pray that it will prove to be worthy of the foundation's vision to put rich theological material in front of people. We also want to acknowledge our brothers and sisters at Clifton Baptist Church, who have strenghtened our faith on the journey home.

In addition, each of us would like to individually thank a few folks:

Jeremy – I'm compelled to mention my parents first, as they put up with a kid whose love for creative writing was sadly not matched with ability. But they never let on they were aware of this gap. They let me live in this illusion long enough to get at least a little traction. But more importantly, they raised me to see the world as God's. I must also mention my wife, Sarah, who gets credit for any work I accomplish and blame for none of it. She is the ground that lets my imagination take off and know where to return.

Cassie – Tyler, thanks for journeying through my illustrations with me and for sharing in the joys and the tears. You offered your eyes, ears, and heart so freely as I navigated the uncharted waters of artistic growth—I love you! Thanks, Mom and Dad, for nurturing my love for the Lord and good books from an early age. Last, but certainly not least, thanks to our family and friends who supported me with prayer and encouragement throughout this whole process.

Our last acknowledgement is the most important, and that is to the one true God, who reveals himself as Father, Son, and Spirit in his Word and as Creator of everything good in his world. In him we live and move and have our being. Lord, may you be honored by what you see here.

A WORD OF WELCOME

The Holy Scriptures are our letters from home.
Augustine

This world is not our home. We live east of Eden and short of heaven. The earlier children understand this, the more sense they can make out of this sad, wonderful place. I hope to shape their vision of the world as a place in-between, to awaken them to the brave journey they must take toward their true home. Their home with God.

The book you are holding is a small imaginative gaze at the limitless wonder of Scripture, in the hope of sharpening your child's taste for one particular theme at the heart of the Bible's story. That theme is the presence of God.

People were made to be with God in the beginning and will find his presence to be their greatest reward in the end. It is what we lost in the tragedy of the fall and what we gain from the victory of redemption. Lost by the first Adam in a garden, regained by the second Adam in a tomb. From Genesis to Revelation, Scripture compels us to see that Jesus is the way—the only way—for sinful people to be welcomed safely back into the presence of the holy God. The very place they were made to be.

Whether you are a child or an adult, let's follow this theme through Scripture like a winding path leading to untold joy at journey's end.

For here we have no lasting city,
but we seek the city that is to come.

Hebrews 13:14

NARRATIVE PERSPECTIVE

Where were you when I laid the foundation of the earth...
when the morning stars sang together
and all the sons of God shouted for joy?

Job 38:4, 7

I attempt to capture the wonder of this unfolding story by utilizing the perspective of two unnamed angels. I was careful not to allow their presence to disrupt the biblical narratives; rather, they serve as a literary device that allows a unique perspective on familiar stories, with certain advantages. Angels have an insider perspective regarding the joy of being in God's presence but an outsider perspective regarding the human drama of being separated from that joy.

Regarding this drama, I should warn that our approach does not sanitize the Bible. We want to inspire children's hearts to courage and alert their souls to cosmic dangers. The world is not safe. Neither is this story. It can't be safe, because it wasn't safe for its main character.

That main character is Jesus Christ. The Bible is about God's hidden plan to bring his lost children home from where they had wandered. He would have to go to where they had lost themselves. To do this, he would become one of them. Jesus was always the plan. The Old Testament squints its eyes looking for him, and the New Testament widens its eyes in awe of seeing him. This book in your hands, this telling of the Bible's story, simply must be about Jesus to be faithful to the original. Jesus is the Alpha and Omega, the opening and the closing lines of the Book.

A JOURNEY HOME

PROLOGUE

Where were you when I laid the foundation of the earth...
when the morning stars sang together
and all the sons of God shouted for joy?

Job 38:4, 7

ELCOME TO OUR STORY.

WELL, IT'S NOT REALLY OUR STORY.

It's yours.

We are just two angels
who have the incredible joy
of being near God.
We get to see him for ourselves
and be so filled with wonder
we find ourselves singing.
We can't help it.

Even if we were allowed
to describe this joy to you,
your language wouldn't hold up
under the weight of glory.
But don't worry.
Your story just might be headed toward
this same joy.
A journey to be near God.
A journey home.

We two angels have watched
  countless people make this journey.
    Their stories will help you understand
      your story.
        But we have to warn you.
          This journey is not safe.
            It never is for those who make it.
            But it is always wonderful.

            You may be wondering our names
              since names are so important.
                But our names don't matter in this story.
                  There's really only one Name
                    you'll need to know.
                      But we'll get there in time.

                      Speaking of time,
                        let's start at the beginning,
                          when everything except God was new,
                            and he was still naming the stars.

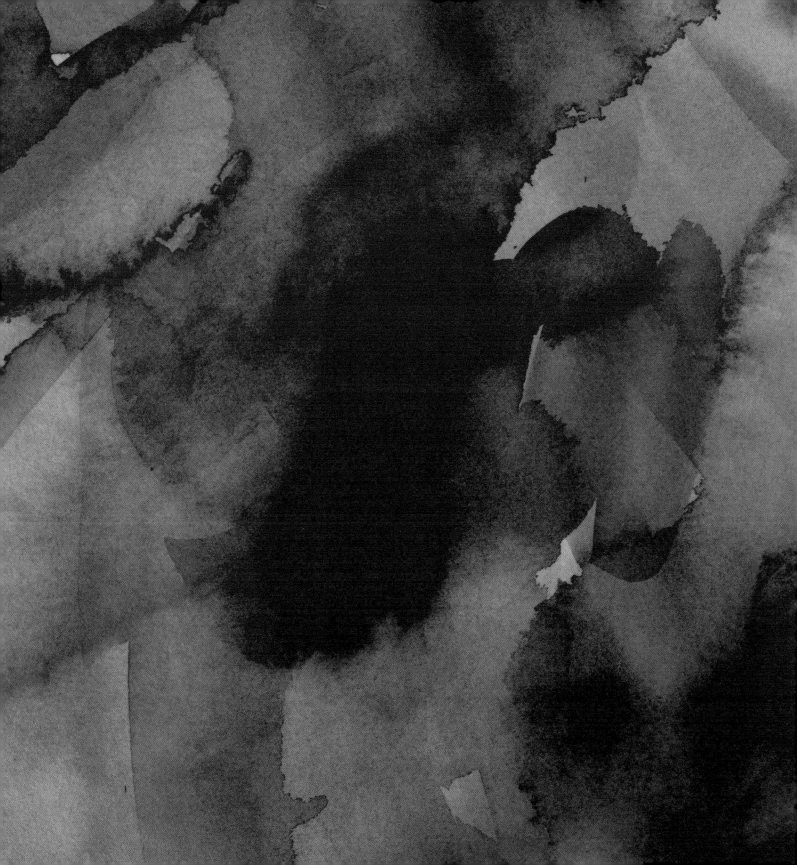

AN EVENING
WALK
WITH GOD

CHAPTER ONE
Genesis 1:1–2:12

By faith we understand that the universe was created
by the word of God, so that what is seen
was not made out of things that are visible.

Hebrews 11:3

E STOOD AT THE EDGE

OF ETERNITY THAT THIRD DAY.
Life was exploding around us
at the sound of his words.

Words that cut through
the swirling darkness
with the vividness of light,
pressing back the emptiness
to make room for life.

Even our bright eyes
  had never seen anything like it.

Somehow the fierce colors of heaven
  were sprouting in this wild, new world.
    As each day passed,
      the words of the Almighty
        made galaxies and frogs,
        stars and daffodils.

      But what took our breath away
      (as you say)
      was his final creation.
      You.
      Well, the first two of you.

You should have seen them together.
Man, woman, and God.
You can't imagine how happy they were.

They took walks together on cool evenings.
Hills blanketed with color,
rivers speckled with jewels,
beauty draped across the sky.

All of it glowed so brightly
because God was there.

14

If you imagine the best day ever—
a weekend trip to the city or the country
with your mom and dad together,
loving each other and loving you—
you'd have to repeat that a million times
to reach one moment
Adam and Eve shared with God,
walking under that tree called Life.

It's hard to imagine for you.
The happiness you know
comes and goes so quickly.
You probably wonder why.

We haven't gotten there yet.
For now, all you need to know is
you were made to be with God.
Your heart is right
when you are home with him.

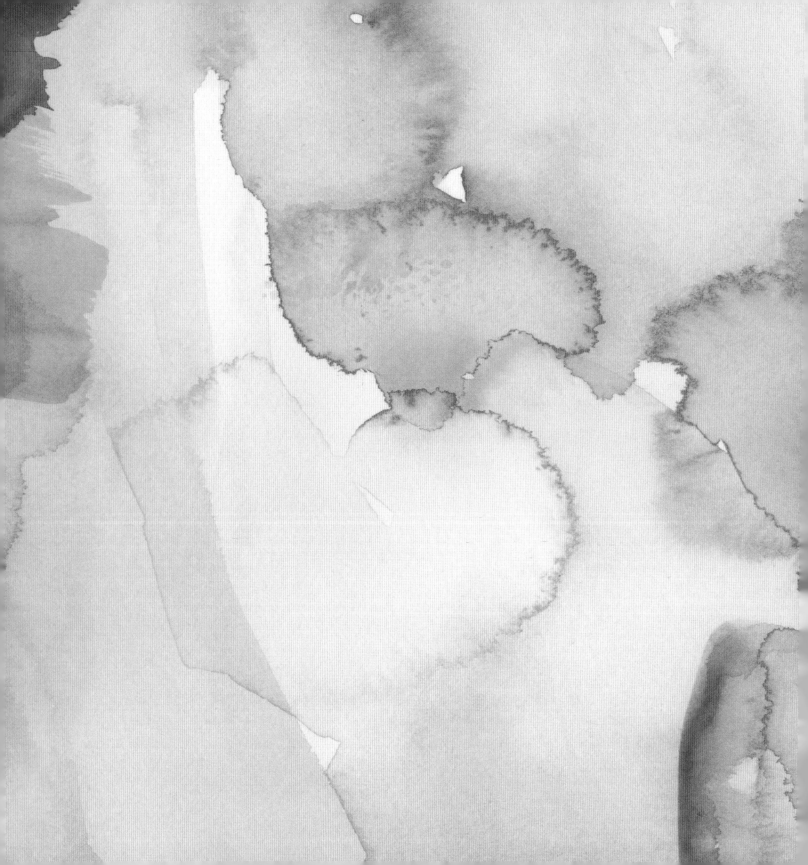

A TERRIBLE
SEPARATION

CHAPTER TWO
Genesis 3

But I am afraid that as the serpent deceived Eve by his cunning,
your thoughts will be led astray
from a sincere and pure devotion to Christ.

2 Corinthians 11:3

E KNEW HIM

RIGHT AWAY.
But they didn't.
The Old Enemy had found
a clever disguise in this new place.
A snake is good for creeping,
and he crept his way between them.
The man, the woman, and God.

"Can you really trust God's words?"

The words made the woman's ears tingle.
Exciting and upsetting at the same time.
She had always believed God was
more than she could ever dream of.

The words made her eyes blink.
The fruit she'd seen a hundred times,
the one God said would harm her,
looked different.

The fruit looked good.
Colorful, tasty, generous.
And God looked bad.
Gray, boring, stingy.

They ate it, and their minds exploded
with something they'd never known before.
A new discovery.
Fear.

Their evening walks with God
used to fill them with delight.
Now the approaching God
filled them with dread.

They had separated themselves
from God.
Their hearts would never unlearn
that terrible separation.
Neither would any of their children's.
Even yours.

You know fear.
And sorry for saying it,
but you know disobedience, too.
Just like every human heart since.

Well, not every human heart.
God promised that one would be different.
With a voice that warmed
the trembling Adam and Eve,
God assured them that
one of their children
would not listen to the snake
but step on it instead.

But none of us knew what that meant yet.

A TERRIBLE
SEPARATION
GETS WORSE

CHAPTER THREE
Genesis 6–9:17 and Hebrews 11:7

Therefore let everyone who is godly
offer prayer to you at a time when you may be found;
surely in the rush of great waters,
they shall not reach him.

Psalm 32:6

OU CAN'T IMAGINE
THE SORROW THAT DAY.
Adam and Eve were devastated.
We were, too.
But none of us could know God's grief.
He keeps many things private.

The misery only got worse.
Adam and Eve ate some fruit,
then their children killed each other.
Their grandchildren did too.
Soon the world was full of hatred.
Those evening walks with God
were long forgotten.

30

Along with God's grief came God's anger.
He decided to punish a world full of sin
by filling it with water instead.
You see, there's no getting around it.
Sin must be punished.

    Yet,
    God told a man named Noah
    how to keep his family safe.
Noah believed God.

It was a special boat God designed.
Strong enough to endure
the enraged waters
and deliver people and animals
 to a clean, new earth.

Then God added a promise
that stretched across the sky.
From then on,
storm clouds would be sliced through
with the colors of heaven,
reminding everyone
that God's mercy will always color his anger
as long as this world remains.

We saw in those waters
how serious God is about people's sin.
But we saw in that ark
how he'll make a way to save them anyway.
It was beyond our understanding.
But, as we said,
God keeps many things private.

THE FIRST CALL HOME

CHAPTER FOUR
Genesis 11:1–9 and 15:1–21

By faith Abraham obeyed when he was called
to go out to a place that he was to receive as an inheritance.
And he went out, not knowing where he was going.

Hebrews 11:8

E WERE SO HOPEFUL

AS NOAH'S FAMILY MULTIPLIED.
We sensed within them
a deep longing for what they'd lost.
A hunger for home.

But when God is not their home,
people try to make their own.

They got together
to build with brick and stone
their own way back to God.
A tower so high it would reach heaven.

But God knew it could never reach.
It could never give what they longed for.
So he scrambled their language,
and they went off wandering.

People did their best to find home,
including one little family
in their own little place.
But God wasn't about to let them settle.

ABRAHAM

SARAH

The Lord told Abraham to leave his place
to go on a journey to a better home.
A home big enough for a world of children.
Only, Abraham and Sarah had no children.
And they were really old.
Not to us, of course.
But older than grandparents to you.

But God always makes a way.
He woke Abraham up in the night
and stretched across the sky another promise.
The stars that God alone can count
would not outnumber Abraham's children.

Abraham believed God,
and that's what God wanted.

Then it dawned on us watching angels—
Ever since Adam and Eve disobeyed,
all of their children disobeyed too.
But God didn't wait for them to obey
to invite them back home.
First he invited them to believe his promise
that home with him is better
than any home down here.

A KNIFE AND A BOY

CHAPTER FIVE
Genesis 22:1–19
and Hebrews 11:17–19

And the Scripture was fulfilled that says,
"Abraham believed God, and it was counted to him
as righteousness"—And he was called a friend of God.

James 2:23

OD IS A GRAND MYSTERY.

HE DOESN'T TELL ANYONE
HIS SECRET PLANS,
and that's why faith is faith.

Abraham received his son,
and laughed so joyfully they called him Isaac.
But then God called, "Abraham?"
"I'm here," he said.

"Take this boy, your only son,
the one you love,
and sacrifice him."

47

God's words were like a knife
to Abraham's throat.
But however they hurt him,
he got up to obey.

He woke his boy for the long journey.
Abraham traveled with two things
that were strange together:
A knife and a boy.

As his son walked with him,
he called, "Father?"
"I'm here," he said.

"Here is the wood and the fire,
but where's the sacrifice?"
Abraham's face was heavy.
"God will provide the lamb, my son."

Abraham's heart was heavy, too.
He found the place and built the altar.
He laid down his boy
and took up his knife.

Then God startled us all
with the boom of his voice,
"Abraham, Abraham!"
"I'm here," he said.

"Don't harm the boy.
I see your faith in your obedience
to give me this son you love."
Abraham dropped his knife
and scooped up his boy.

When he looked up he laughed.
Near them the whole time
a ram had been caught in a bush by the horns.
Abraham now saw
what he before had to trust.
God provided a sacrifice in his son's place.

God is indeed a grand mystery
who can always be trusted.

A DREAM AND
A WRESTLING MATCH

CHAPTER SIX
Genesis 28:10–22; 32:9–32

My soul clings to you;
Your right hand upholds me.

Psalm 63:8

JACOB

ESAU

HE BOY WHO CAME
OFF THE ALTAR GREW UP,
AND HAD TWO BOYS OF HIS OWN.

One of Isaac's boys was particularly tricky.
The little crook would do anything
to get what he wanted.

Jacob wanted for himself the home
God had promised grandpa Abraham.
So he tricked his older brother Esau
into trading him God's promise
for a bowl of stew.

Esau figured out he had been tricked,
and Jacob ran away.
He had to use a rock as a pillow,
but somehow had the best dream ever.
A ladder from ground to sky,
higher than that old failed tower
everyone had worked so hard to build,
carried angels up and down
into the burning glory of God's place.

"Like I told Abraham and Isaac,
I will give you a home for your future family
where I will live with them," God said.

Fear and joy woke Jacob up.
"I have found where God lives!"
Jacob went on his winding way,
not knowing yet what all this meant.

Years later, he had another odd encounter.
A silent man came out of nowhere
and tried to wrestle Jacob to the ground.
Jacob realized what he was up against
when the man only touched Jacob's hip,
and it stopped working right.
Jacob knew only God had such power,
and he held on even tighter.

"Let me go," the no-longer-silent man said.
Jacob grunted in response,
"I won't let you go until you bless me."
"Very well. Your name is now Israel,
since you wrestled with God
and got what you wanted."

Jacob suddenly sat alone, blinking,
"I met God again and didn't die!"
But he did limp.
Jacob learned that meeting God
was the most wonderful
and the most dangerous thing
a person can do.

You just might find this out
for yourself before the end.

AWAY FROM HOME
BUT NEVER ALONE

CHAPTER SEVEN
Genesis 37 and 39–46

As for you, you meant evil against me, but God
meant it for good, to bring it about that many people
should be kept alive, as they are today.

Genesis 50:20

OD'S PROMISES WERE ALIVE.

JACOB HAD TWELVE SONS,
Reuben, Simeon, Levi, Naphtali, Issachar, Asher, Dan, Zebulun, Gad,
Judah, Benjamin,
and Joseph.

All those boys meant a lot of sharing.
But they didn't share everything.
Jacob gave Joseph a coat so colorful
it caught the eyes of his brothers.
So his brothers decided
to share a little pain with Joseph.
They grabbed him and sold him to strangers,
then ruined his coat with blood.

Joseph was taken to a place called Egypt,
a place where no one knew God.
And even when he did all the right things,
they put him in prison,
forgotten and alone.

But he wasn't really forgotten and alone.
God was with him.

One night God sent alarming dreams
to the king of Egypt.
But the king could not understand the warning.
No one in Egypt could.
Except Joseph.
He was the only one who knew God.
Joseph told the king God would stop the rain,
No water meant no food.
So the king told Joseph
to save enough food
to keep everyone alive...

...including Joseph's brothers.
They left home for Egypt
because they were starving.
Joseph could have let them.
But, as we said, God was with Joseph,
and God forgives even cruel people.

Not only does God forgive their cruelty,
He turns that cruelty inside out.
What his brothers meant for evil,
God meant for good.
If Joseph hadn't been sent far from home,
the drought would have killed everyone.
Only God was clever enough to plan that.

No one knew then that God
was hinting at some distant day
when he would use a far worse sin
to save far more people,
including you.

JOSEPH

GOD HEARS
A BABY CRYING

CHAPTER EIGHT
Exodus 1:1–22; 2:1–10

By faith Moses, when he was born, was hidden
for three months by his parents, because they saw that the child
was beautiful, and they were not afraid of the king's edict.

Hebrews 11:23

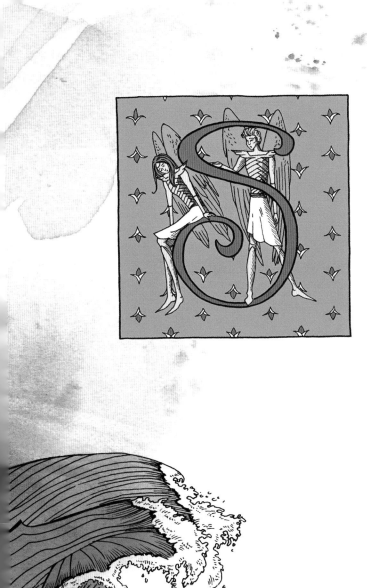

SOMETIMES GOD KEEPS HIS PROMISES
BY USING POWERFUL THINGS.
Sometimes he uses regular things.

To save his people from Egypt, he used both.

He started with the most regular thing
you can think of,
a baby crying.
And another very regular thing,
the soft spot ladies have for crying babies.

Even there in a strange land,
Jacob's big family had grown into a nation,
a nation of strangers in Egypt.
And the king didn't want them taking over.

Pharaoh told the two ladies
who delivered the newborns
to kill them right away.
These two ladies feared the king.
But they feared God more,
because they knew he was the true King.
So they disobeyed.
And the Lord was quite pleased.

71

Another lady also had compassion
on her baby boy.
She put him in the river,
but not to drown him.
She and her husband believed
by putting baby Moses in a basket,
God would somehow carry the boy
to safety.
But God had a better plan,
to carry all his people out of there.

So he used another lady,
a little one.
Moses' big sister loved her baby brother
and followed him down the river
to watch over him.

73

All baby Moses had to do was cry,
and the only lady both important enough
and kind enough to help
heard him.
A princess of Egypt
loved this baby from the river,
but she needed a nurse to care for him.

So Moses' big sister told the princess
she knew the perfect lady to raise Moses.
His own mother.
So baby Moses went right back to his family,
who raised him to know God's promise
to give his people a home of their own.

WORDS OF FIRE

CHAPTER NINE
Exodus 2:23–25; 3:1–15; 4:1–13

Let me hear what God the LORD will speak,
for he will speak peace to his people.

Psalm 85:8

MOSES

OSES GREW UP SECRETLY WANTING HIS PEOPLE OUT OF EGYPT, so he tried to fight for them.

The problem was, no one followed him.
So he ran away to lead sheep instead.

Out in the silent hills,
Moses' eye caught something amazing.
A bush that burned but wasn't burnt.
It was God,
a patient, consuming fire.

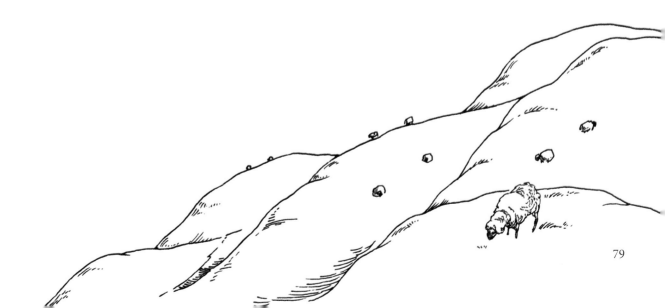

"Do not come near with dirty sandals.
This place is holy
because I am here.
I have heard my children crying.
I will bring them to the home I promised.
Go tell Pharaoh to let them go."

"But I'm nobody," Moses replied.
"I will go with you."
"But what's your name?" Moses questioned.
"I am who I am."
"But they won't believe me," Moses said.
"I will give you amazing power."
"But I can't talk very well," Moses stammered.
"Who made your mouth?"

At first we couldn't understand
why Moses was so scared.
Then we realized he was still learning
what all God's children eventually learn:
It wasn't up to him.
It was up to God.

81

God doesn't just use regular things
to keep his promises.
He uses amazing things, too.
A staff turned into a snake,
A river turned into blood,
Frogs and gnats rising out of water and dust,
Sickness and sores, hail and locusts,
Pitch darkness.

Only God could do all those things
to save his people from slavery to Pharaoh.

But something far worse was coming,
the curse of all who refuse to listen to the Lord:
the darkness of death.

SAFE AND SOUND IN
THE DEADLY NIGHT

CHAPTER TEN
Exodus 11:1–10; 12:21–34

For Christ, our Passover Lamb,
has been sacrificed.

1 Corinthians 5:7

GOD WAS VERY SERIOUS.
"I'M ABOUT TO BRING A PLAGUE
that will break Pharaoh's heart
and everyone else's with it.
Tonight I am bringing my Destroyer."

We were silent.
We knew what that meant.
"At midnight, he will go through the streets
and kill the firstborn in every house.
Everyone will cry harder
than they ever have before."

Moses didn't speak.
So God spoke some more.

"But I will make a way
to keep the Destroyer
from harming my children."

The children of Israel listened to God.
They took their best lambs
and killed them
and felt very sad,
since the lamb didn't do anything wrong.

They streaked the blood on their doors
and hid in their houses,
just like the Lord told them to.
When they heard screaming in the streets
and saw they were safe in their homes,
they realized what was going on.

The lamb had died instead of them.
The Destroyer, who was killing so many,
had passed over them.

"Get out of here!" Pharaoh cried to Moses.
And in the middle of the night,
the children of Israel grabbed their things
and exited Egypt so fast
the dough for their bread
didn't even have a chance to rise.

None of us knew then
that this Passover was a small one
compared to one that was coming,
when a better Lamb would be killed
so God's children wouldn't have to be.
This was an even bigger plan
that came from deep in God's heart,
stretching over thousands of years
so that countless more people
could be safe in the deadly night, too.
Including you.

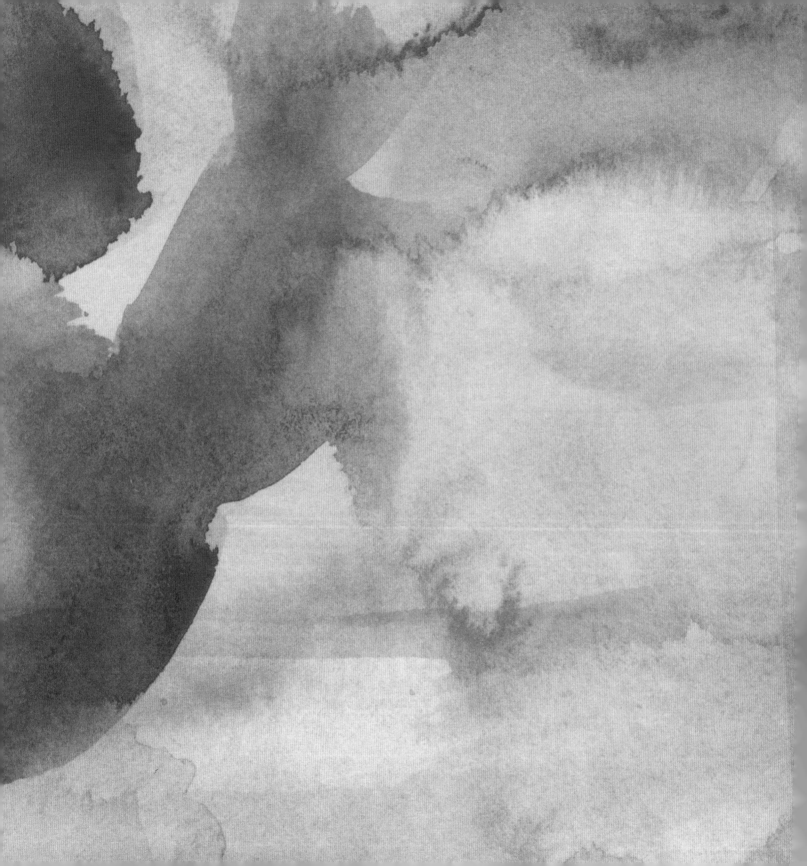

THE DANGER OF
BEING
NEAR GOD

CHAPTER ELEVEN
Exodus 32 and 33

For you have not come to what may be touched,
a blazing fire and darkness and gloom...
But you have come...to Jesus, the mediator of a new covenant.

Hebrews 12:18, 22, 24

OD'S PEOPLE EXITED EGYPT GLORIOUSLY, ONLY TO FIND THEMSELVES in a bleak desert, where they found a place even more dreadful: a mountain that stormed and trembled because the Lord was there.

This terrible mountain
was different from the happy garden.
The difference was not in God.
He had always been holy.
The difference was in people.
Their sin made God's holiness dangerous.

This mountain was a puzzle
we angels hadn't been able to piece together:
God had promised to be with his people,
but how could a holy God be near sinful people
without destroying them?

But the love in God's heart
always has a plan.
He called Moses to come up alone
into his presence,
which was like the fiercest blazing fire,
the purest darkness,
and the brightest light.

"I am giving you my good commands,
but as I speak my people already disobey.
I cannot go with them
because I would have to destroy them."

Moses fell on his face and cried,
"But remember your promise
to Abraham, Isaac, and Israel.
To give their children a place with You.
If you do not go with us,
we are worse than dead."

The Lord was pleased with Moses' prayer.
Moses was defending God's people,
not because they were good.
Moses knew they were rotten.
His only reason was that God himself
had promised to save them.

Moses prayed so boldly
because he knew how deeply God loved his children.
The puzzle was coming together.
God was making it possible for one person
to enter the danger of his presence
to plead for sinners.
And God would listen with joy in his heart
because he loves to show mercy,
to welcome sinners safely home.

GOD LIVES
WITH HIS CHILDREN

CHAPTER TWELVE
Exodus 40 and 1 Kings 8:12–9:9

Come, let us go up to the mountain of the LORD,
to the house of the God of Jacob, that he may teach us his ways
and that we may walk in his paths.

Micah 4:2

HE PLACE WHERE GOD IS MUST BE BEAUTIFUL,
AND IT MUST BE HOLY,
for God is both.

If God were to go with his people,
they would need to build him a place
that would always remind them
of the dangerous beauty of God's holiness.

The people made a tent as God commanded,
from the beautiful things of earth.
Shining gold, rippled wood, delicate linen.
Blue, purple, scarlet red.
An altar, an ark, a mercy seat.
Carved and cast with artistic passion.

Later, God's people would build
a permanent house.
A temple built by an army of craftsmen,
a grand house of cedar and gold,
trees and fruit and flowers masterfully crafted,
lions and oxen captured in bronze,
pillars towering overhead,
statues of the unseen angels.
All built on top of a mountain called Zion.
Heaven and earth came together
in one golden meeting place.
Immaculate beauty.

Except that it would be stained
by animals dying inside.
Blood sprinkled, poured, burnt.
A terrible business for such a beautiful place.

But it made people see with their own eyes,
hear with their own ears,
smell with their own noses
the stark difference between
the beauty of God
and the penalty of sin.

107

God was showing sinners the old puzzle.
He could not be near them,
or they would be destroyed.
Unless.

Unless their sin was paid for
by a replacement.
For now, it was an animal.
But God knew the blood of bulls and goats
cannot take away sins.

The people did not yet fully understand
that a better replacement would be needed.
A person.
One that could do what no animal could:
be holy like God,
and thus be a truly worthy sacrifice
who could take away the sins of the world.

And that is exactly what God planned to do
so that people could return
to the beauty of being near him.

FINDING
A HOME FOR GOD'S PEOPLE

CHAPTER THIRTEEN
Deuteronomy 12 and 28
and Joshua 1:9; 6:1–27

I am the LORD and there is no other,
besides me there is no God.

Isaiah 45:5

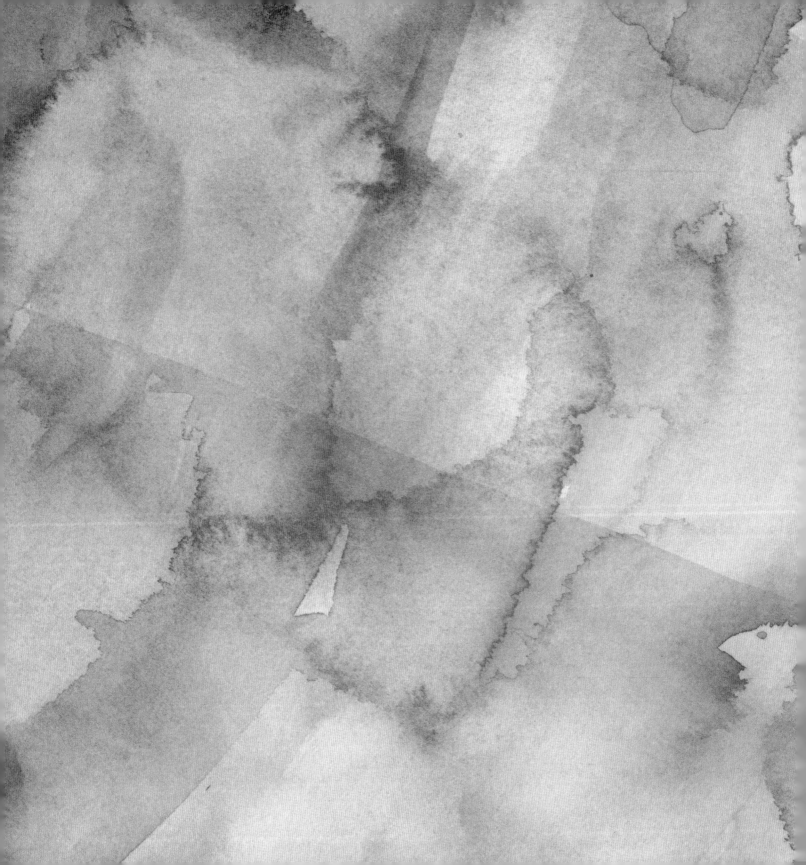

HE LAND GOD

HAD PROMISED HIS PEOPLE
**was already full of other people,
people who worshiped different gods,**
gods they'd imagined for themselves.

A god carved in wood was easy to worship
because it can't tell anyone what to do.
A living God is a speaking God.
The true God tells his people what to do
so they can know how life works best,
even when they imagine they know better.
Or maybe especially then.

As Moses' life came to an end,
he left Joshua to finish leading Israel home.
Joshua knew they would only get there
by trusting the words of God
over the dumb idols who spoke nothing.

"Be strong and courageous.
For I am with you wherever you go.
So keep my words.
Think about them day and night.
Love them with all your heart.
Follow them in everything you do.
And I will be with you."

When Joshua heard the Lord speak,
he treated God's words as better than gold.
At first, so did all the people of Israel.
But soon these words became too much,
and they found the gods of gold
that didn't tell them what to do.

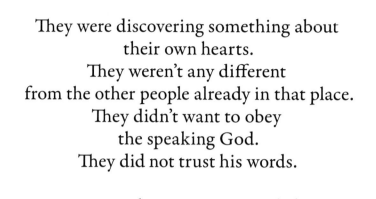

They were discovering something about
their own hearts.
They weren't any different
from the other people already in that place.
They didn't want to obey
the speaking God.
They did not trust his words.

We angels were again puzzled.
We thought Israel had finally found home.
But home is not a place to settle their bodies.
It is a place to settle their hearts.

What makes the human heart
long for home so desperately,
but be too restless to settle?

THE GIANT OF BRONZE
AND THE BOY OF FAITH

CHAPTER FOURTEEN
1 Samuel 17

For by you I can run against a troop,
and by my God I can leap over a wall. This God—his way is perfect;
The word of the LORD proves true.

Psalm 18:29–30

HE DAYS JOSHUA LED ISRAEL CAME TO AN END,

**AND THE PEOPLE WANTED A NEW LEADER.
A king.**

Now, most kings think they are
the mightiest person in the land.
But God appointed a king in Israel
who knew he wasn't.
God chose someone who learned as a boy
that true strength was only in God's promises.

The boy David went to visit his brothers at war.
But when he arrived,
they weren't preparing for battle.
They were shaking with fear.
Goliath.
A man who seemed to be made of bronze,
gleamed large like an angry sun,
with weapons like some brutal machine,
and a filthy mouth cursing God's people.

DAVID

"Who is this dirty Philistine
that he should defy the armies of God?
I will fight him," David said.
The warriors of Israel stared at the boy.
But David was young enough
to believe the promises of God
over what his eyes saw.

The giant saw David and laughed,
"You think I'm a dog scared of a stick?
Come here, kid.
I'm going to feed you to the buzzards."

David replied,
"You have your weapons with you,
but I have my God with me.
God is going to feed you to the buzzards,
so everyone knows
God is with his people."

David was not a warrior.
He had only a boy's weapon, a sling.
With that sling, he flung one little stone
past Goliath's great spear,
past his massive shield,
past his gleaming helmet,
and into his forehead.
The bronze giant fell like a bronze statue.

That day everyone saw God's presence
was deadly to the enemies of his people.
King David would not forget this.
Neither should you.
God would prove countless times again
that those who trust his promises
should fear nothing.

THE MUSIC OF
BEING CLOSE TO GOD

CHAPTER FIFTEEN
Psalms 16; 22; 32; 42–43; 139

Sing and rejoice, O daughter of Zion,
for behold, I come and I will dwell in your midst,
declares the LORD.

Zechariah 2:10

E ANGELS ARE CLOSE TO GOD.
WE SEE HIS BRIGHT GLORY
in ways that would
burn your eyes out.

But people can be close to God
in ways we can only dream of.
They sing of this closeness
with a song we can only listen to with envy
but never produce ourselves.
Because it's the song of faith.

It took King David a lifetime to learn this song,
as it does for all those who believe,
and therefore sing.

Sometimes the song is happy,
delighting in the nearness of God
more than anything else
in all the world.

Sometimes the song is sad,
wondering where God went
when life goes suddenly dark
and hope lies somewhere out of reach.

Sometimes the song is fearful,
anxious about God's acceptance
when sin seems so shameful
it could never be forgiven.

Sometimes the song is hopeful,
confident that God's heart burns
with mercy so intense
no sin can extinguish it.

Sometimes the song is a sigh,
sometimes a groan,
other times a laugh,
still others a shout.

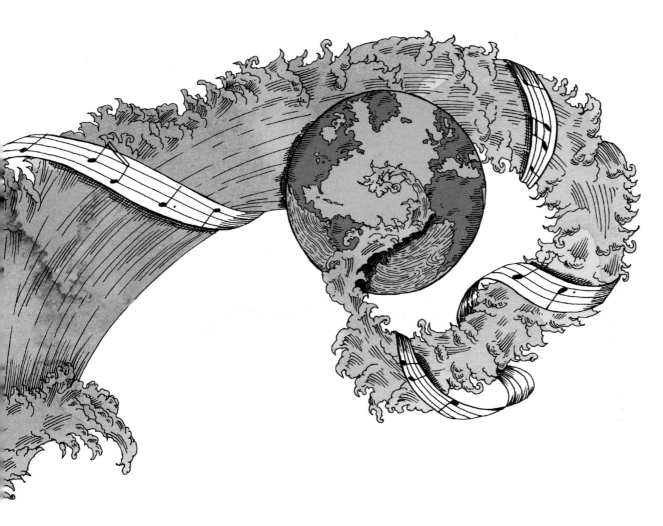

It's a song that starts when the Lord
first captures a heart
with his love.
And, we've been told,
it will go on being sung
forever.

GOD'S HOUSE EMPTIED

CHAPTER SIXTEEN
Jeremiah 7:8–15
and Zephaniah 1:10–18

Let all the inhabitants of the land tremble,
for the day of the LORD is coming; it is near, a day of darkness
and gloom, a day of clouds and thick darkness!

Joel 2:1–2

A DAY LIKE THIS HAD
NEVER ENTERED OUR MINDS.
THE DAY OF THE LORD
no one wants to repeat.

King David had a heart like God's.
But his sons and grandsons didn't
inherit that heart.
Some of them loved God,
but most of them loved whatever god
served their purposes.
And they led everyone else to do the same.

They ignored God's words
and forgot his heart.
They thought they could keep God
alongside their other gods,
since they still had the temple.
They thought the temple was a sure sign
that God was with them.

But God sent prophets to tell them
He would take the temple away,
because they had made it a joke
and didn't care if he was in it or not.

God refused to live in a land
where they worshiped other gods,
where they hurt poor people,
where they stole and murdered,
where they did not honor marriage.

So the day came when God judged his people.
It was a terrible day.
A day of thick darkness.
A day of fire, swords, and weeping.

Before this day, countless times
God had ordered us angels to defend his people.
But this day, he gave no such order.
God allowed the enemies of his people
to destroy the temple
and carry them away.

We stood by and watched bewildered.
We knew God would not forsake his people.
But on this day,
we had no idea how.
Thankfully, this day would not last forever.
Another day would come.
The Lord had promised.
And he never breaks his promise.

THE
MYSTERIOUS
SERVANT

CHAPTER SEVENTEEN
Isaiah 52:13–53:12; 54:7–8

He himself bore our sins in his body on the tree,
that we might die to sin and live to righteousness.
By his wounds you have been healed.

1 Peter 2:24

HE TEMPLE
WAS RUINED.

THE LAND WAS DESOLATE.

THE PEOPLE SUFFERED

far away from their home,
slaves to the gods they had chosen to serve.
The curse God had sworn on them
for their disobedience was upon them.
But even his own curse on them
did not dim God's desire to bless his people.
For some deep, private reason,
He still loved them.

So into that dark time, God spoke
of a mysterious servant he would send.
Like a new tree growing out of an old stump,
He would be everything Israel failed to be.
He alone would deserve the reward
that God had promised to those who obey.

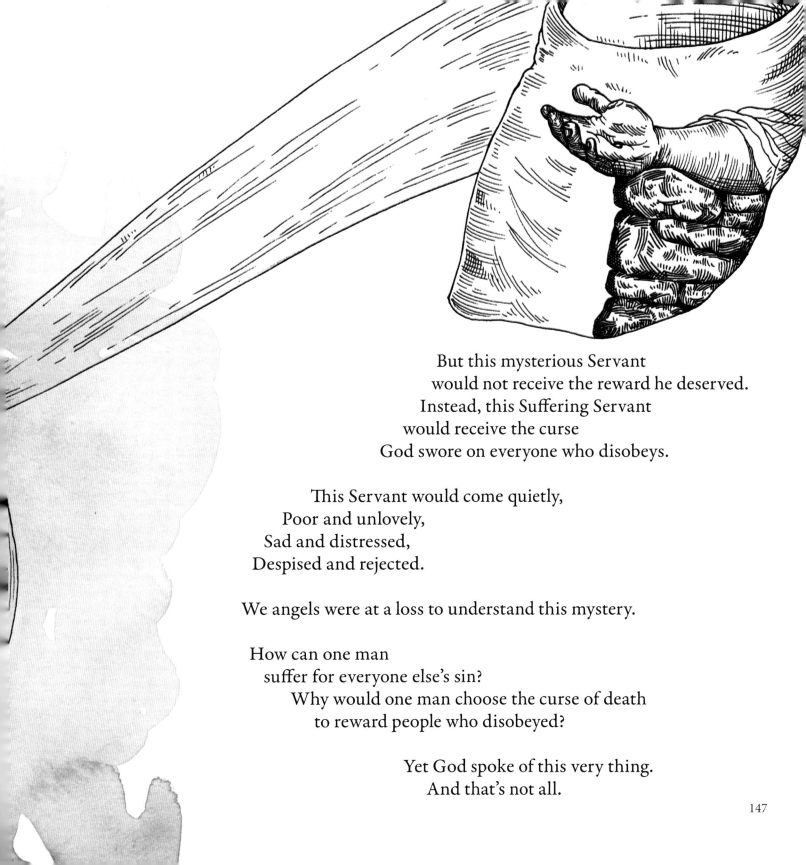

But this mysterious Servant
would not receive the reward he deserved.
Instead, this Suffering Servant
would receive the curse
God swore on everyone who disobeys.

This Servant would come quietly,
Poor and unlovely,
Sad and distressed,
Despised and rejected.

We angels were at a loss to understand this mystery.

How can one man
suffer for everyone else's sin?
Why would one man choose the curse of death
to reward people who disobeyed?

Yet God spoke of this very thing.
And that's not all.

147

This servant would rise from the darkness,
breaking the curse of death,
welcomed with the joy of God
because he gave himself as a sacrifice
for others.
His reward, the one thing he would ask for:
that his wounds would heal his people
from all over the world.

Instead of the curse
God had sworn on them all,
they received the reward
God had promised him alone.

What a mystery.

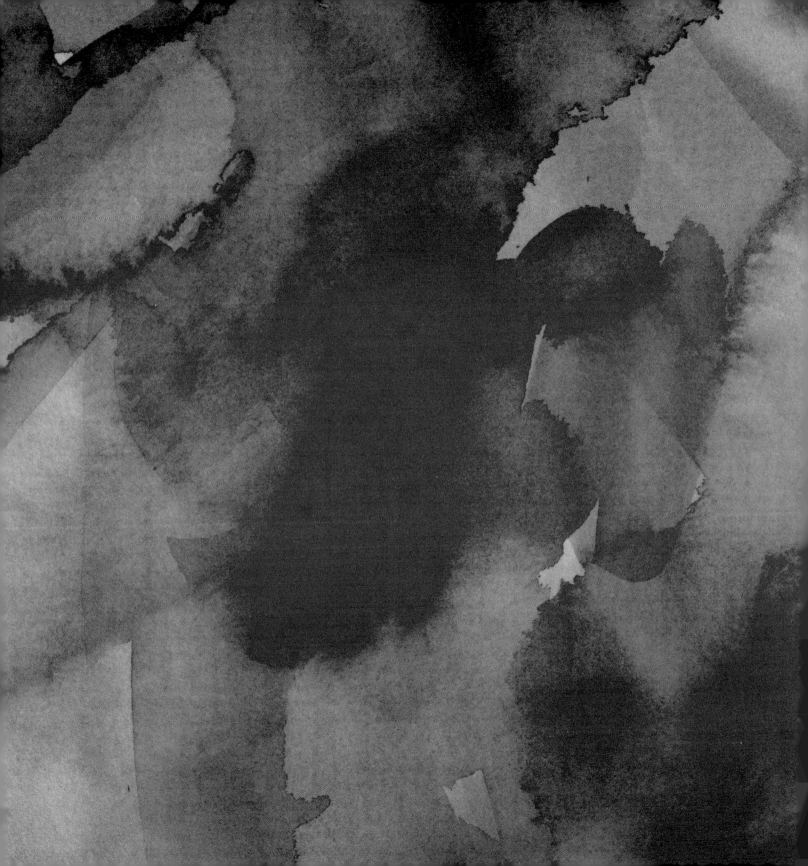

THE SILENCE OF GOD

INTERMISSION

To you, O Lord, I call;
my rock, be not deaf to me, lest, if you be silent to me,
I become like those who go down to the pit.

Psalm 28:1

HE SILENCE OF GOD IS DARKNESS.

For many lifetimes,
God ordered us to stop
carrying messages to his prophets.
The words his people needed
to find their way home
did not come.

Darkness is
the silence of God.

THE
BABY WITH
TWO NAMES

CHAPTER EIGHTEEN
Matthew 1:18–25 and Luke 1:26–2:21

But when the fullness of time had come, God sent forth his Son,
born of woman, born under the law, to redeem those who
were under the law, so that we might receive adoption as sons.

Galatians 4:4-5

HE FIELDS AND HILLS
OF ISRAEL WERE STILL.
BUT THE EXPANSE OF HEAVEN
was brimming with activity.

God was going to break his silence,
and he was going to do it
by speaking in a way he never had before—
by crying out in the night
as a baby.

Never had heavenly beings been so astonished,
even at creation itself.

This baby would be called by many names,
but he was introduced with two in particular.
The most important names ever given
to a child in your world.

Gabriel was sent from God's presence
to a frightened young lady named Mary.
He said to her,
"Don't be afraid. The Lord is with you.
You will have a baby boy,
and your son will be God's Son.
He is called Jesus
because he will save his people from their sins."

The sound of her son's name
awoke something deep in Mary.
She said,
"May his Word stand true."

Gabriel then went to Mary's fiancé, Joseph,
and lit up his dreams.
"Don't be afraid to take Mary as your wife.
She is already carrying God's Son inside her.
He is called Immanuel
because God himself has come to his people."
Joseph awoke and obeyed.

We angels had learned enough by then to know
these two names are only good news
when they go together.
God With Us is dangerous news for sinners,
unless he also comes as God Is Salvation.
Together, these names are the gospel.

This baby with two names
would be the best news
ever spoken before or since.

THE BABY KING IN DANGER

CHAPTER NINETEEN
Matthew 2:1–18

Now therefore, O kings, be wise;
be warned, O rulers of the earth.
Serve the LORD with fear, and rejoice with trembling.

Psalm 2:10–11

T'S QUITE DANGEROUS FOR A BABY KING

TO BE BORN INTO A WORLD
full of kings already.

Jesus was born in a place
that had a king already.
So this king was surprised
when some sky watchers came from far away,
following a mysterious star
that announced the birth of an ancient King,
a King who would rule over all kings.

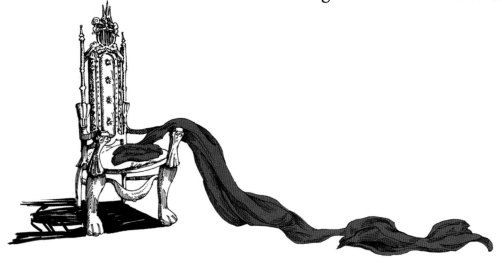

This did not make King Herod happy.
So Herod tried to trick the wise men
into spying on Jesus.
But the wise men did not spy on Jesus.
They worshiped him.
They had read of this baby in the sky,
written by a hand
much mightier than Herod's.

168

Herod was enraged enough
to hunt down any baby boy he could find.
But he never found Jesus
because Joseph and Mary had taken him far away.

King Herod was nothing more than a serpent
in the hands of the Old Enemy,
who was still hunting God's children
across the ages.

We were baffled
why God would put his Son in such danger,
in a world where mothers wept.
Apparently, for Jesus to save helpless people,
He had to become helpless himself.

JESUS BEGINS TO
UNDO THE SEPARATION

CHAPTER TWENTY
Mark 2:1–12

If this man were not from God,
he could do nothing.

John 9:33

DO YOU REMEMBER THE JOYFUL GARDEN WHERE EVERYTHING was right?

Jesus grew up outside that garden.
Instead of joy,
He saw brokenness all around him.
When he became a man,
he began doing something about it.

One particularly broken man
had friends who brought him to see Jesus.
People were crowded all around Jesus,
waiting to see.
But these friends didn't wait and see.
They believed already.

So they ripped through the roof to get to Jesus,
and laid their friend at his feet.
"Take heart, my son, your sins are forgiven,"
Jesus said.

The folks who were there just watching thought,
"Who does he think he is?
Only God can forgive sin!"
But no thought can hide from Jesus.

Jesus looked over with narrowed eyes,
and saw their hard hearts.
"What's easier, to forgive sins or heal bodies?"
The watchers couldn't answer.
Neither could the friends of this broken man.

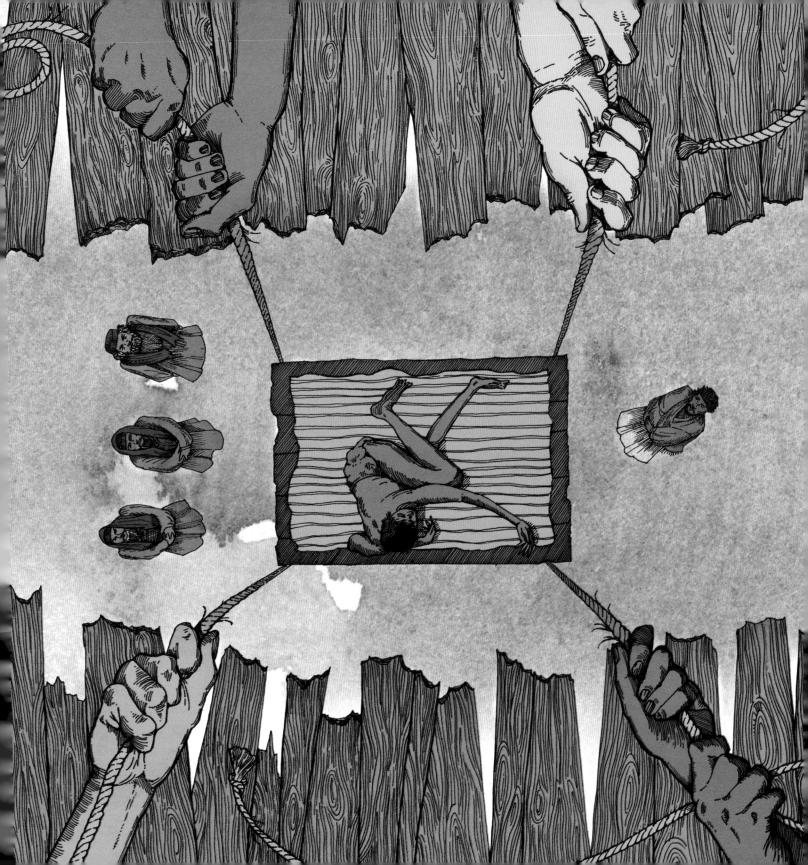

Jesus looked down with gentle eyes,
and saw his wrecked body.
"I say, rise and walk."
Then the man who could not walk
walked.

Jesus was showing everyone that where he is,
both sin and brokenness
lose their place.

It's probably hard for you to imagine
a place where no one is broken or sick,
weak or dying.
A place where no one is jealous or mad,
mean or selfish.
But that's only because it's hard for you to imagine
how wonderful it is to be around God.
And Jesus is God.

JESUS GOES TO
UNCLEAN PEOPLE

CHAPTER TWENTY-ONE
Numbers 5:1–4
and Luke 5:12–16

So Jesus also suffered outside the gate
in order to sanctify the people
through his own blood.

Hebrews 13:12

IN A WORLD OF SICKNESS AND DEATH,

no one was allowed to pollute the place where God is.

Israel lived under the Law of Moses,
which said that people with disease
must be put outside the city
so that they wouldn't touch anyone
and pollute them too.

So people with gross diseases
would have to show the priests,
and they would no longer be welcomed
until they became clean.

The problem was
no one could make them clean.
Not the priests,
not the doctors,
not themselves.

So when Jesus came to unclean people,
the Law said not to touch them
or he would be unclean too.

But Jesus knew his were the only hands
that could make them clean.

A peeling leper.
A bleeding woman.
A dead little girl and her broken father.
By touching them,
Jesus took their defilement.
He removed their uncleanness
so that they could be welcomed back
into the place where God is
and death is not.

The happy people who were whole again
could not have known that Jesus
would soon be put outside the city to die,
unclean with sin he never did.
He did this to make not just their bodies clean,
but their hearts as well.
So they could be welcomed back with God
forever.

CHILDREN

GET TO BE NEAR JESUS

CHAPTER TWENTY-TWO
Matthew 18:1–6
and Mark 10:13–16

See what kind of love the Father has given to us,
that we should be called
children of God.

1 John 3:1

E ANGELS HAVE NOTICED THAT PEOPLE LOVE

TO FEEL IMPORTANT.
Even those who follow Jesus.
Even they would sit and argue about
which one of them was the greatest.

So Jesus called a child to stand in the middle.
"Unless you change to become like this child,
you cannot be with me in my Kingdom."
The disciples were confused.

Later on, some parents brought their children
to see Jesus.
The disciples were annoyed and told them
Jesus had more important people to see.

When Jesus heard this, he was angry.
"Let the children be near me.
Don't you dare stop them.
Children understand better than you
how to be close to me."

The disciples looked embarrassed.
They stood helplessly
as Jesus gave all his attention to the children.
He was showing his followers
they were not more important.

Children don't try to be
important to Jesus.
And that's exactly why
He welcomes them.

To be near to God
you cannot bring anything with you
to impress him
or to make you special in his eyes.
You are not special to God
because of your obedience to him.
You are special to God
because of his heart toward you.

The Lord loves to show mercy
to those who know they need it.
And children are very good
at knowing their need.

JESUS IS
THE PLACE TO MEET GOD

CHAPTER TWENTY-THREE
John 2:12–23 and 14–17

And I saw no temple in the city,
for its temple is the Lord God the Almighty
and the Lamb.

Revelation 21:22

**OU REMEMBER
HOW IMPORTANT
THE TEMPLE WAS.
IT WAS THE ONE PLACE
heaven and earth met,**
the one place God dwelled with his people.
Jesus loved the temple
because he loved being near God.

But when he saw what was going on
in the temple,
he became angry.
The temple leaders were making people
pay money
to be near God.

So Jesus braided a whip
and drove out their pricey animals
and poured out their bins of coins
and forced the crooks out of God's place.

The temple leaders were furious:
"Who do you think you are?"

Jesus turned to them slowly.
"Tear this temple down,
and in three days I will raise it up again."
Everyone laughed.
"It took us 46 years to build this place.
And you'll rebuild it in three days?"

But they didn't know
what we angels had figured out.
Jesus wasn't talking about that temple
made of stone by human hands.
He was talking about himself.

Jesus would die and rise again
as the new temple,
the one place
sinful people can safely meet God
with their sins paid for.

Jesus would never make people pay
to be near God.
They would not need to buy animals
to sacrifice every year.
He would be their sacrifice,
once and for all.
Without cost.

The leaders did not like Jesus
and did not want the people to listen to him,
so they decided to put an end to him.

THE MOST TERRIBLE
SEPARATION
OF ALL

CHAPTER TWENTY-FOUR
Luke 22:41–44

For our sake he made him to be sin
who knew no sin, so that in him we might become
the righteousness of God.

2 Corinthians 5:21

LINDING DARKNESS

SWEPT IN LIKE AN UNEXPECTED STORM
over the events of Jesus' life.
Suddenly angry men grabbed Jesus,
whipped his body,
beat his head,
nailed his hands and feet
to a hastily assembled cross.

We were alarmed and confused.
God had never abandoned any of his children,
no matter how dark life became.
There we stood at God's command,
legions and legions of angels
ready to spring to the aid
of their Creator,
who was suffering
a pain he alone could bear.
But God did not send us to save his Son.

Jesus looked up to heaven for help,
but the sun had hidden its face
because God had hidden his.

"My God, my God,
why have you
forsaken me?"

We had never heard the Creator wail.
But Jesus cried for the loss of something
none of us—human or angel—could comprehend.
Jesus, who had walked closer with God than any man,
was being exiled farther from God than any man.
The most terrible separation of all.
Something grave had come between them.

Sin.
But it was not Jesus' sin.
You'll pardon us for saying so, but we must.
The sin was yours.
And yet the curse was his.
The curse of sin is death,
and death came for Jesus.

As he slumped silently down,
a sound split the air
from the temple not far away.
The curtain that had separated the holy God
from sinful people
was torn from top to bottom.

That frayed curtain
was Jesus' parting message
that he had been forsaken
so that you could be welcomed.

THE SECOND ADAM
AND A NEW PEOPLE

CHAPTER TWENTY-FIVE
John 20:1–23
and Romans 5:15–17

But you are a chosen race,
a royal priesthood, a holy nation,
a people for his own possession.

1 Peter 2:9

E STOOD AT THE EDGE

OF ETERNITY THAT THIRD DAY.

**Life was exploding around us
at the sound of God's words.**

Even our bright eyes
had never seen anything like it.
Somehow the fierce colors of heaven
had erupted in the eternal darkness of hell.
Death was torn open
because a sinless man cannot stay dead.

Jesus was alive.

Eternity awoke in a hillside cave.
Jesus was no longer a lifeless corpse.
He was a breathing man.
God had retrieved his Son
to bring him back,
to bring him near.

Now Jesus wanted to be near his people too.
He spoke the name of Mary as she wept,
and woke the women from their sorrow,
and walked with his disciples on the road,
and their hearts burned with wonder,
burned with hope.

Grief melted to joy.
Fear melted to courage.
Doubt melted to faith.

"Do not be afraid.
You are now my brothers and sisters.
I'm sending you out of here, but not alone.
The Holy Spirit will go with you.
I will go with you.
The Father will go with you."

Jesus had done it.
He was the second Adam.
Only, he had obeyed God perfectly.
Jesus was the first
of a new race of people,
loved by the Father and kept by the Spirit.
God and people together again.

Then to prove people could now be with God,
Jesus went up through a sky no longer dark,
where he now lives
forever.

GOD'S NEW HOUSE

IN A DARK WORLD

CHAPTER TWENTY-SIX
Ephesians 3:9–12,
Titus 2:11–14, and 1 Peter 2:4–10

So then you are no longer strangers and aliens,
but you are fellow citizens with the saints
and members of the household of God.

Ephesians 2:19

OU MIGHT THINK ANGELS KNOW EVERYTHING.

WE CERTAINLY KNOW SOME THINGS

better than you.
But others are a mystery to us.
We shine with the light of supernovas.
But about some things,
we're in the dark.
Until God reveals them to us.

One of the greatest mysteries
he uncovered for us
was something you may find quite ordinary—
a profound secret called
the church.

God had been planning all along
to build himself a house
where he would dwell on earth.
But it wasn't the old temple,
made of lifeless stones.
It was a new temple,
made with living stones.

It wasn't the old temple,
where people were purified
by animal sacrifice for a time.
It was a new temple,
where people are purified
by Jesus' sacrifice for all time.

The people of God no longer go to a temple.
They are the temple,
since God lives inside them,
making them holy like he is.

God silenced angels and devils
by revealing the incredible mystery
that his new house
is not a place,
but a people.

A people both saved by grace from their sin
and trained by grace to overcome their sin.
A people who act like God
in a world that doesn't.

In a gloomy world,
dark and stained,
millions of temples,
bright and clean.

BEAUTIFUL, DIRTY FEET

CHAPTER TWENTY-SEVEN
Matthew 28:16–20 and Romans 10:14–17

How beautiful upon the mountains are the feet of him
who brings good news, who publishes peace,
who brings good news of happiness, who publishes salvation.

Isaiah 52:7

YOU'LL HAVE TO PARDON US FOR POINTING OUT

THAT OUR FEET ARE MUCH CLEANER

than yours.
Our wings of light
carry us wherever God wishes
without ever touching the ground.

But God says
that the glory of our wings
cannot approach
the profound beauty
of dirty feet.

Blistered, worn-out feet
that walk through mud and jagged stones
would carry God's people
to bring good news
to places once dark
with the silence of God.

Nations that had once been God's enemies
would hear the words of Jesus
from the lips of his people.

Dirty feet would fulfill
the promise of the shining stars
God had stretched before Abraham.

People all over the world
would be welcomed into God's family
in the same way Abraham
was welcomed into God's family,
by hearing and believing.

People far away brought near.
Aliens welcomed as citizens.
Strangers adopted as family.
Rich or poor,
brown or beige,
child or adult,
man or woman.

Perhaps God could have chosen
to proclaim this good news with angel voices.
But he didn't.

He chose to relay it from the lips of people
with beautiful, dirty feet.

JESUS IS ALWAYS NEAR

CHAPTER TWENTY-EIGHT
Philippians 4:4–7
and Hebrews 4:14–16

My soul clings to the dust; give me life according to your word!
My soul melts away from sorrow; strengthen me according to your word!

Psalm 119:25, 28

JESUS KNEW WHAT IT WAS LIKE

TO LOOK UP AT THE GLOOMY SKY AND WISH HIMSELF AWAY **because fear and temptation**
seemed to be everywhere around him.

He knew what it was
to go to bed distressed
and wake up weary to face another day.
He knew what it was
for Satan to urge him
with a thousand pleasures apart from God.

But he kept a secret within,
and this secret kept him.
He knew his Father was always close enough
to hear when he prayed
and to speak in his Word.

Believing this kept the teeth of fear from sinking in.
Believing this broke the fangs of temptation.

232

Jesus knew that without God near,
he never would have made it.
And he knows his followers need the same
if they are going to make it.

So he taught them to pray to their Father,
and he taught them to dwell in his Word.
Prayer is approaching the throne of God;
Scripture is receiving the word of God.

In both,
  God shapes his people's hearts
after his.
  He changes the way they see things,
    gives them a new way to respond
      to the fear and temptations
        swirling around them.

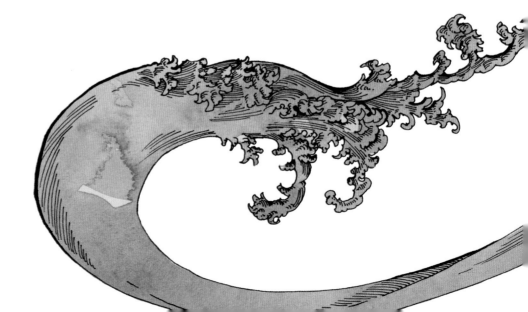

Grace to calm the turmoil of fear,
when your worry feels like
a storm inside you.
Grace to break the power of sin,
when you ache with desire
for what you know is wrong.

In his years under the sun,
we saw Jesus wrestle with fear and temptation
and rise victorious over both.
So now he can help his people,
who look up at the gloomy sky
and wish themselves away.

One day his people will be whisked away
to a brighter place.
But until then,
you will never be too far away
for Jesus to hear
and to help.

FINALLY HOME WITH GOD

CHAPTER TWENTY-NINE
Revelation 21–22

And the city has no need of sun or moon to shine on it,
for the glory of God gives it light, and its lamp is the Lamb.
By its light will the nations walk.

Revelation 21:23–24

DAY IS COMING THAT WILL BEGIN
WITH THE LAST DAWN,
so powerful and clear,
it will end nighttime forever.
Those who belong to Jesus
will awake to find
the darkness was just a passing thing.

That eternal morning,
pure as winter and warm as summer,
mature as autumn and fresh as spring,
had always been their home.
For they were children of the light,
children of God.

That bright
        tomorrow
            will end the terrible separation
                that sent you out of the first garden.
                    For this day dawns on a new garden.

            A garden that is a city
                and also a temple,
                    a better country,
                        a holy mountain,
                            a new earth,
                                a new heaven.

color, language, and nation,
nder the light of this new sun.
can't imagine how happy they will be.
Boys, girls, and God.
The happiness they know will not come and go.
It will only increase more and more,
since they will finally know
what they were always meant to be:
To be with God
and to be like God.

THE
UNFINISHED
CHAPTER

CHAPTER THIRTY
Hebrews 11:13–16

For people who speak thus make it clear that they
are seeking a homeland.... Therefore God is not ashamed
to be called their God, for he has prepared for them a city.

Hebrews 11:14, 16

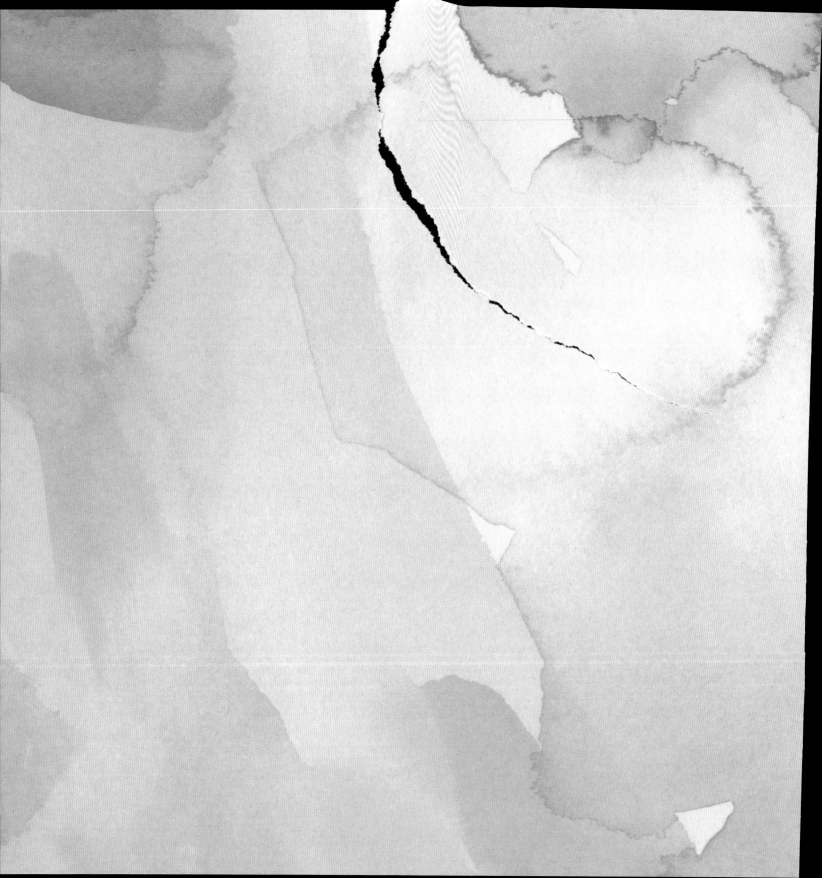

**OU MAY THINK
YOU'RE HOME NOW.
BUT AS FAMILIAR
as this place is,**
this world is not your home.

We've noticed that most people
try to convince themselves it is.
But their hearts know better.
In both the wonder
and the trouble
of this place,
their hearts ache
for the garden
they lost.
Their first home.

This ache will drive you all your life
to find the home you know
 is somewhere out there.
   The question is
    which home will you find?

    Sin promises you a thousand homes,
       a thousand different gardens
          full of color,
             but empty of God.
                These gardens are yours for the taking.
                   Your place. Your way. Your home.
                      But you will find
                         their colors bright for only a moment.
                         A home without God
                            is a garden without water.
                            Everything dies.

                         Like every person born outside Eden,
                          your heart prefers dead gardens,
                          because dead gardens are safer
                          than the presence of the living God.
                          Or are they?

Remember when the serpent tricked Eve?
You would be bitten by death.
But Jesus knew those fangs were for him.

Remember the storm-tossed ark?
You would have sunk under those raging waters.
But Jesus knew he'd drown under sin's punishment.

Remember the little boy on the altar?
You would be lost from those who love you.
But Jesus knew he was the ram that replaces you.

Remember the deadly night of the Passover?
You would have died like an Egyptian.
But Jesus knew his blood would keep you safe.

Remember the animals in the temple?
You would have never stopped paying for your sin.
But Jesus knew he'd be slaughtered once and for all.

Remember the mysterious servant?
You would have gone astray like a lost sheep.
But Jesus knew he'd be crushed for the sins of his people.

Remember the baby King hated by all kings?
You would have been hunted by the Evil One.
But Jesus knew he'd be attacked instead.

Remember the cross?
You would have died and been lost.
But Jesus knew his descent into death would raise you.

255

Jesus was bitten, drowned, slaughtered,
crushed, hunted, and killed
so that you wouldn't have to be.
He left his home
to accomplish everything necessary
to make you holy
so you can join him
in a holy place
he calls home.

This home is also yours for the taking.
It will cost you nothing.
It will cost you everything.

Turn your journey there.
Trust the promises of Jesus.

God with us.
Us with God.
Home.

POSTSCRIPT

Dear Children,

I'm no angel. I'm just the author of this book you're holding.

But because I'm no angel, I can tell you that I was a lost kid who found his way home. Or maybe I should say, the way home found me. Jesus is more than able to find you, too.

What Jesus is looking for is not the good kids, the ones who do everything right. There's really no such thing. He's looking for the kids who know they are not good, the ones who understand that their sin makes them unworthy to be with him.

Are you one of those kids? If so, you need to hear a story Jesus told about himself.

"What man of you, having a hundred sheep, if he has lost one of them, does not leave the ninety-nine in the open country, and go after the one that is lost, until he finds it? And when he has found it, he lays it on his shoulders, rejoicing. And when he comes home, he calls together his friends and his neighbors, saying to them, 'Rejoice with me, for I have found my sheep that was lost.' Just so, I tell you, there will be more joy in heaven over one sinner who repents than over ninety-nine righteous persons who need no repentance" (Luke 15:3-7).

Jesus loves to take kids like you, sweep them up in his arms, and carry them home. On the way, he reassures them a thousand times of his heart toward them. He assures them they are loved with a love as limitless as God himself. And he assures them they are forgiven with a forgiveness that makes the God who forgets nothing forget their sin.

If you want that love and forgiveness, it can be yours. There's really no special password or secret code you have to know. Jesus tells us in two simple terms how to respond to him.

Repent. If you are sorry for your sin and want to turn away from it, ask God to forgive you.

Believe. If you believe Jesus is stronger than your sin and can make you righteous like him, trust him to save you.

That's it. If you still need help (and you will) find people who love Jesus Christ and ask them to show you in Scripture how to follow him. Maybe that would be your parents or grandparents. Maybe that's a teacher or a coach. They will help you find a church that loves the Bible, so that you can keep following this story all the way home.

I pray that by the amazing grace of the Lord Jesus, I will see you there.

Until then,

Jeremy